BE A WINNER

Other Books by James R. Sherman

How to Overcome a Bad Back

Rejection

Get Set . . . GO!

Middle Age Is Not A Disease

Escape to the Gunflint

•

In the **DO IT!** Series

Stop Procrastinating—DO IT!

Patience Pays Off

No More Mistakes

Plan For Success

Farewell To Fear

BE A WINNER

JAMES R. SHERMAN

Pathway Books

First Edition, December, 1989
Copyright © 1989 James R. Sherman
All Rights Reserved

Library of Congress Catalog Number
87-062218

International Standard Book Number
0-935538-11-9

Printed in the United States of America

Pathway Books
700 Parkview Terrace
Golden Valley, Minnesota 55416
(612) 377-1521

To: Ralph B. Cloward, M.D.
there is no one better.

CONTENTS

PREFACE   ix

INTRODUCTION

A Definition   1
Why People Strive to Succeed   2
The Elements of Success   5
The Rest of the Book   14

WHAT WINNERS AVOID

Fear   18
Pessimism   18
Bad Habits   19
Procrastination   19
No Control   20
No Learning   20
No Direction   21
No Commitment   21
No Motivation   21
No Self-Esteem   22
No Perseverance   22
Poor Perception   23
Wishful Thinking   23
Reliance on Luck   24
Subject to Stress   24
Need for Gratification   25
Poor Interpersonal Skills   25
The Road Ahead   26

HOW TO BE A WINNER

Win a Few   27
Be Happy   28
Visualize   29
Persevere   29
Prioritize   30
Be Prepared   32
Take Control   32
Be Courageous   32
Take a Chance   33
Know Yourself   33
Be Responsible   34
Commit Yourself   35
Build Character   35
Relate to Others   35
Think Positively   36
Plan Your Future   37
Broaden Your Base   39
Cultivate Your Mind   39
Control Your Emotions   40
Be a Problem Solver   40
Go For It   41

A PLAN OF ACTION

INDEX   45

PREFACE

I learned something about winning when I was running hurdles in high school. Back in the fifties, at a meet in Marshall, Minnesota, the track conditions were so bad that the officials had to reduce the number of runners in each heat from five to three. That increased the number of heats from two to four. I ended up as the only runner in the fourth heat.

You can't imagine how excited I was, knowing that I was finally going to win a race, even though I was running against myself. I had never won before because I was so darned slow. Then, at the last minute, some turkey who knew he could beat me and make the finals, entered the race and was added to my heat. There was no way I was going to let that jerk eclipse my moment in the sun.

I never ran so hard in my life. Neck and neck the two of us plodded our way to the finish line. Finally, with him breathing down my neck, I felt the tape break across my chest. I was a winner, and I still have my faded ribbon to prove it. It was a great experience, but it taught me a lesson that I've never forgotten. I first saw it written down in a book by the American humorist George Ade. He said:

"Anyone can win, unless there happens to be a second entry."

That's as true for running the high hurdles as it is for trying to drag yourself out of mediocrity. In the second case, you're running against yourself. And the only way you can win is by beating the person inside of you who's holding you back.

This book is for people who want something better than what they have right now. It doesn't tell you how to stomp on other people to get what you want. It tells you how to do your best and be the best in whatever you do. It tells you how to be the first one across the finish line, whether you're running against a turkey or trotting down the pathway of life all by yourself.

The strategies in this book have helped me reach a level of success that has made me very happy. They can help you do the same, if not more. I hope you enjoy reading it as much as I enjoyed writing it.

James R. Sherman, Ph.D.

INTRODUCTION

Damon Runyan, the American journalist, said, "The race isn't always to the swift, or the battle to the strong, but that's the way to bet."

There is a difference between winners and runners-up, as you will see throughout this book. If you think you're in the back of the pack and want to be a winner, then pay close attention. Because this book is going to teach you how to get out of your rut and into the sunshine of success.

If you're going to be a winner, you'll have to know what winning is all about; what it means to win and why winners stand out among their peers. That's a fairly easy task and it's pretty much what this section of the book is all about. Once you get past the definitions, you'll come up against some basic suggestions for changing your behavior. That's when you'll have to roll up your sleeves and really get to work.

A DEFINITION

Winners are people who are consistently able to reach ideal levels of accomplishment through their ability, persistence, and hard work.

In contrast to winners are those people who consistently fail to reach common standards of performance in business, social endeavors, or life in general.

Winners and nonwinners are not differentiated by wealth, power, or fame, but by the ratio between what they are, and what they could be if they worked at it.

A winner's success in life is more a matter of desire and concentration than it is of talent and opportunity. Success is attained by simple means

1

and the exercise of ordinary qualities, especially common sense and per-severance.

Winners live each day as if it were going to be their last. Their biggest task is not to get ahead of others but to surpass themselves. They try hard to live positive, constructive lives *now* instead of waiting until some vague and indefinite time in the future.

WHY PEOPLE STRIVE TO SUCCEED

People are motivated by their wants, needs, and desires; all of which reflect things they think they're missing. People who know what they want out of life are usually more motivated than those who only have vague ideas of who they are, what they are, or where they're going.

Highly motivated people know what they're good at and what they like to do. They know their strengths and weaknesses, and they're aware of most of the risks and opportunities that await them. They are realistic about the future, and they have specific goals and objectives they think will get them there.

Individuals react not only to the people, objects, and conditions in their environment, but also to their thoughts, emotions, and bodily needs. They obviously can't satisfy all their needs, so their self-concept helps determine the particular needs they elect to pursue at any one time. Their choice depends on the people they're with, the situation they're in, and what they're thinking about at the time their needs are felt.

Psychologist Abraham Maslow thought people's needs could be arranged in a hierarchy, from basic to higher level needs as shown here.

1. *Physiological Needs:* hunger and thirst
2. *Safety Needs:* security, order, and stability
3. *Belongingness and Love Needs:* affection, identification, and affiliation
4. *Esteem Needs:* prestige, success, self-respect, and achievement
5. *Self-Actualization Needs:* self-esteem, self-fulfillment
6. *Cognitive Needs:* knowledge, awareness, understanding
7. *Aesthetic Needs:* beauty, balance, serenity

Maslow believed that once people were fed, they would be off in search of success or some other form of interpersonal satisfaction. Sometimes winners and nonwinners want the same things. The difference comes in the way their wants are expressed and the way in which they are satisfied. Here are some of the more common wants that people have.

1. *Acquisitions:* the desire to acquire, possess, or hoard material possessions
2. *Affiliations:* the desire to be associated with, or be in the presence of other people
3. *Altruism:* the desire to help others
4. *Curiosity:* the desire to explore and investigate one's environment, seek novel stimulation, and strive for knowledge
5. *Power:* the desire to control other people or objects, to get their obedience, to compel their actions, and to determine their fate
6. *Prestige:* the desire to be highly regarded by one's associates

People seek to satisfy their wants according to the way they feel about their world and the people they find in it. Some will seek power over prestige. Some will join a country club instead of a labor union. Some will collect seashells, others will collect classic cars.

Wants, needs, and desires are terms that are often used interchangeably to describe perceived deficiencies. Needs are generally thought to be more essential than wants or desires, although in many cases, the difference is merely semantic.

The satisfaction of one's wants, needs, and desires can be risky, depending on how intense they are and how hard it is to satisfy them. Winners will usually go for it in spite of the obstacles. Duffers will usually stand pat until the odds are better.

Take a moment now and reflect on the things you want most in life. Then turn to page 4 and put down 10 wants, needs, or desires that you think you have to satisfy to be successful. Describe any obstacles or risks that might keep you from being satisfied. Then come back here and look at some of the elements that make up what we call success.

MY TEN MOST IMPORTANT WANTS, NEEDS, AND DESIRES

1. _____

2. _____

3. _____

4. _____

5. _____

6. _____

7. _____

8. _____

9. _____

10. _____

Obstacles or risks I anticipate

_____

_____

_____

_____

THE ELEMENTS OF SUCCESS

Bessie Anderson Stanley won a contest, sponsored by the *Brown Book Magazine*, for coming up with a definition of a successful person. She said a winner was someone "who has lived well, laughed often, and loved much." These three characteristics, living well, laughing often, and loving much, will give you a broader understanding of what it means to be a person who has achieved a praiseworthy position in their lifetime.

LIVING WELL

Here are some of the major elements of "living well" as suggested by Wilferd A. Peterson in his book, *The Art of Living*.

Giving

Successful people like to share the gift of life by giving some or all of the following:

1. *Gifts of Time:* companionship, assistance
2. *Gifts of Words:* guidance, inspiration, encouragement
3. *Gifts of the Mind:* ideas, dreams, projects, poetry, purposes, principles, inventions
4. *Gifts of the Heart:* joy, love, kindness, sympathy, tolerance, forgiveness, understanding
5. *Gifts of the Spirit:* faith, peace, prayer, vision, beauty, inspiration

Winners know that the only "true" gift is a portion of themselves; not necessarily money, but whatever they have of sympathy, encouragement, and understanding for their fellow human beings.

They give love to their friends; tolerance to their opponents; forgiveness to their enemies; honor to their parents; guidance to their children; commitment to their spouses; respect to themselves; charity, benevolence, and love to all those in need; and a smile to everyone.

The way they give shows their character more than the gift itself. They give as they receive; cheerfully, quickly, and without hesitation.

The more they give, the more they live. They know that if they give to the world the best they have, then the best will come back to them.

Guiding

Successful people try to draw out the best in others by setting good examples. They reach out to those under them and try to help them climb the ladder of success. They trust people, believe in them, and have faith in them.

Winners serve as role models for others by knowing what they're doing and having the initiative and imagination to carry it out. They're not interested in having their own way but in finding the best way. They work hard, and are successful because of their application, resoluteness, and perseverance.

They are dreamers, doers, and people of action. They are self-starters with open minds who create plans and set them in motion. They set their minds on attainable goals while at the same time helping others reach higher levels of performance.

Working

Successful people see work as a blessing, not a curse. They believe they can express themselves through their work and make a contribution to human progress. They know that being a slave to a job and just putting in time does not bring the joys of work, but rather the disappointment of a wasted life. They pour their spirit into their work without hesitation, making it a reflection of their faith, integrity, and ideals.

Winners know that all growth depends on activity, that there is no development physically or intellectually without effort, and that effort means work. They also recognize the great healing power of work. They know that work eliminates fear, worry, loneliness, and discouragement and is the key to happiness.

Reading

Mark Twain said, "The person who doesn't read good books has no advantage over the person who can't read them."

Winners know that reading is a major factor in their success. But it is not just *what* they read, it's *what they comprehend* that makes them strong. They seek to touch the lives of other great thinkers by burying themselves in their books and combining their thoughts with those of the authors. They read as much as they can about a wide variety of subjects. They read something new every day, drawing from humor, poetry, the teachings of great philosophers, and the findings of renowned scientists. They read to link the past, present, and future in a full sweep of world history. They look for new sources of wisdom, knowledge, and inspiration to enrich their spirits, add new dimensions to their lives, and give them new insights about their world and the people in it.

Thinking

Successful people set no limits on the power of ideas. They know that the greatest events of any age are its best thoughts, because thoughts find their way into action.

They think for themselves in the search for truth. They use their imaginations to create and their critical minds to judge. They approach problems intuitively and logically, by observing, analyzing, considering, and questioning. They strive to develop a mature mind without losing the simplicity of childhood.

Winners know that their happiness depends upon the quality of their ideas. Life has taught them how to think pleasant thoughts, but thinking has taught them how to live pleasant lives.

Winners know their minds are like parachutes and will only function when they're open.

Henry Ford, the American automaker, knew how much effort went into thinking great thoughts. He said, "Thinking is the hardest work there is, which is probably why so few people engage in it."

Relaxing

Winners recognize that relaxed living is productive living, so they take time for relaxation and meditation. They manage their minds, bodies, hearts, and spirits as efficiently as they manage their businesses. They exercise, eat and drink in moderation, and maintain a sense of humor. They don't take themselves so seriously that they can't laugh at themselves now and then.

They know how to live with the stress of daily living. And they know how to bend under its force without breaking. They think thoughts of peace and quiet and tranquility. They seek environments where they can sap the strength of nature's calming power.

Persisting

President Calvin Coolidge said, "Nothing in the world can take the place of persistence. Talent will not; nothing is more common than unsuccessful people with talent. Genius will not; unrewarded genius is almost a proverb. Education will not; the world is full of educated derelicts. Persistence and determination alone are all-powerful. The slogan 'press on' has solved, and always will solve, the problems of the human race."

Winners know that if success is worth having, it's worth pursuing. Once they commit themselves to a plan of action, they resist all distractions and do everything they can to accomplish their intended goal.

Being Aware

Successful people maintain a sense of oneness with life by staying mentally alert to everything around them. They are curious, observant, and imaginative. They stretch the range of their senses by taking time to look, listen, and comprehend.

They have developed a deep sensitivity through which they suffer, know tragedy, and maybe die a little, but through which they also experience the grandeur of life. They identify with the hopes, fears, and longings of others, and they seek to understand and help others whenever they can.

Winners have discovered the mystic power of silence and the inner voice of intuition. They see life steadily and they see it whole. They stand in awe and wonder of life's unexplained mysteries and seek to build an ever-increasing bank of knowledge about the world in which they live.

Being Happy

Winners know it's not the place or the condition, but the mind alone that can make them happy or miserable. They know they'll never be unhappy as long as they keep their minds full of rich thoughts, their hearts full of rich emotions, and their bodies occupied with productive endeavors.

They are happy because they have something to look backward to with pride and something to look forward to with hope. They're pleased with what they've been able to achieve, but they're also motivated to do better. They put their hearts in their work, then bask in the afterglow of knowing they did a tough job and did it well.

They meet the problems of life with cheerfulness and enthusiasm. Feelings of goodwill, tolerance, and understanding are second nature to them. Not so much from doing what they like to do, as from liking what they have to do. It's easy for them to find happiness in little things, like a baby's smile, the song of a bird, a letter from a friend, or the sights, sounds, and smells of nature.

The French courier Francois Rochefoucauld knew how little it took to gladden the heart of a winner. He said, "Few things are needed to make the learned person happy, but nothing satisfies the fool."

Being One's Self

Winners are not pretentious because they know there is little to pretend to. They know who and what they are and they take pride in their selfhood. They accept themselves, respect themselves, live their own lives, and follow their own stars. They make the most of what they have and always strive to be better.

They know their potential, their spiritual heritage, their strengths and weaknesses, and their aims and purposes. They know what they can and cannot do. They delight in fanning the spark of possibility into the flame of achievement.

Being Thankful

Successful people are grateful for their good fortune and accept their talents and abilities as obligations to be invested for the common good. They believe in the *Golden Rule* and do to others as they would have others do to them.

They show their thanks for beauty by making the world more beautiful. They give thanks for health and strength by giving care and reverance to their bodies. They express their thanks for creative ideas by making creative contributions to human progress. And they demonstrate their thanks for each day by living it to the fullest.

Being Friendly

Winners know that friendship is more than just a kindly smile or an outstretched hand. It's the spiritual inspiration that comes from discovering that someone else believes in them and is willing to trust them as a friend.

They know that the only way to have a friend is to be one, so they set examples that serve as inspiration to others. They encourage instead of discourage. They respond in positive ways to other people's dreams and aspirations. They lift people up with tolerance, forgiveness, and understanding, instead of casting them down with pretense, hypocrisy, and insincerity.

They also know that friendship has great mathematical powers. It doubles their joy and divides their grief.

Being Efficient

Successful people know that goals, objectives, and efficient methods make any task easy, agreeable, and successful. So they work very hard at finding the best, easiest, and quickest way of getting things done. And if they can't find a way, they'll make one. That usually means doing one thing at a time.

They know that if they practice doing something for a while, it will get easy. If it gets easy, they'll enjoy doing it. If they enjoy doing it, they'll do it more than once. And if they do it regularly, it will become a constructive habit that will help them be successful.

Being Adventurous

Successful people see themselves as being surrounded by infinite possibilities for growth and achievement. Their curiosity and thirst for adventure prompts them to seek new experiences, explore new horizons, and try new ways of living and thinking.

They cultivate the flexibility they need to adjust to changing patterns of life and they build up the courage they need to wrestle with new and difficult problems. They read new books, court new friends, take up new hobbies, and adopt new viewpoints. Their success comes from keeping their hearts young, their spirits strong, and their expectations high.

Staying Young

Winners know people do not grow old, they get old by not growing. They know that youth is the season of hope, enterprise, and energy, to a nation as well as to an individual. They know that the hopes and dreams that occupy the minds of young people are previews of the character of the next generation.

They see the blending of young and old as providing a purifying release from the worn and stained hardness of older life. They know that if they can keep something of youth in their aging bodies, they will never grow old in their minds.

They keep their minds active and alert by searching out the precious friendship of young people, from whom they gain their inspiration and hope. By staying flexible, adaptable, open-minded, and young at heart, they know they will be constructively busy for the rest of their lives.

Living Forever

Winners do not see the final test of their lives as how *much* they lived, but how *well* they lived. Their purpose in life is not just to be successful, but to be useful and productive, and to have someone else say that it made a difference that they lived at all.

They see immortality — to never die or be forgotten — as the fulfillment of their existence. So did the Greek philosopher Aristotle who said, "Whatsoever there be within us that feels, thinks, desires, and animates is something celestial, devine, and consequently, imperishable."

Mastering Fear

Successful people have fears like everybody else. They succeed because they are brave enough to confront the dark side of fear with the bright light of reason and knowledge. They are willing to accept challenges and enthusiastically seek adventures that the weakhearted avoid.

They are not afraid of failure. They realistically accept it as part of life. They know they cannot be successful in everything they do, so their philosophy is to do the best they can, make the most of what they have, and accept what comes.

They know that every failure can be a step toward success. Every detection of what is false can steer them toward what is true. Every trial can expose some tempting form of error. Even bitter and crushing defeats can provide the foundation for a rousing success. With an outlook like that, fear doesn't stand a ghost of a chance of getting the upper hand.

Having Patience

Winners act quickly and decisively, but with patience, because they know success takes time.

They have studied the methods of highly successful people, and they have incorporated those techniques into their own hopes, dreams, and aspirations for the future. They have committed themselves to reaching a list of realistic goals and objectives. They have learned to identify the obstacles that stand in the way of their success, and they have learned to deal with those obstacles in a calm, cool, and collected manner.

Winners universally endorse the first part of Bessie Stanley's definition of success by living well. They also subscribe to the power of humor and the benefits of laughter.

LAUGH OFTEN

Successful people know that whenever people smile, but much more when they laugh, something is added to life itself. They know laughter provides relief from stress and is the perfect antidote to anxiety and depression. Laughter is also extremely valuable, as noted by Charles Lamb, the English essayist. "A laugh," he said, "is worth a hundred groans in any market."

They fill their lives with the sunshine of good cheer, and always laugh *with* others, not *at* them. They laugh at what people do without laughing at who they are. They think something is funny when no one blushes with embarrassment, when no one carries away an ache, when nothing sacred is made to appear common, when no one's weakness provides another one's laughter, when profanity is not needed to make it funny, when no child is brought to tears, and when everyone can join in the laughter.

They refuse to take either life or themselves too seriously. They look at the funny side of difficulty and are able to handle problems more effectively by tossing them around, handling them with a light touch, and taking a playful attitude toward them.

They know that a sense of humor helps maintain a proper perspective of what's important and what's not. They deflect attacks and move away from interpersonal confrontations by using their sense of humor to good advantage. They have found that humor is an excellent way of bringing people together. Comedian Victor Borge, who has made millions of people laugh, has often said, "Laughter is the shortest distance between two people."

They know that by being cheerful, they will do more in the same time, will do it better, and will preserve in it longer than people who are sad or sullen. They know that laughter improves people's complexion, adds spring in their step, and puts drops of sunshine and brilliance in their eyes.

Winners are not concerned when critics complain about their lighthearted approach to life. Instead, they take comfort in the words of the English author J. H. Leigh Hunt who said, "Leaves seem light, useless, idle, wavering, and changeable. They even dance. Yet God made them part of the mighty oak. So He has given us a lesson; not to deny stoutheartedness within because we see lightheartedness without."

A light heart, as winners know, is also a heart full of love.

LOVE MUCH

Successful people are rich in admiration and love, and free from envy and hate. They feel good about the goodness of others, and they love with great generosity of heart.

They have discovered that there is more pleasure in loving than in being loved. They never judge rashly and never interpret the actions of others in a bad light. They bear other people's burdens without complaint and show compassion toward their agony without restraint. They bury other people's weaknesses in silence, and proclaim their virtues from the mountain tops.

Winners draw their happiness and love from the happiness and love of others. They never seek a reason for their love, they just give it. And sometimes they worry about not having given enough.

They know that there is more to success than the qualities of living well, laughing often, and loving much. They know they can also be successful if they leave the world better than they found it, if they fill their niches and accomplish their tasks, if they look for the best in others and give the best they have, if they gain the love of children and the respect of intelligent adults, and if they never lack appreciation for earth's beauty or fail to express it.

THE REST OF THE BOOK

Pause for a moment before you move on to the next section, and think about the elements of success you just read about. Then turn to pages 15 and 16 and respond to the six categories that are listed. It will give you an idea of how involved you are with the elements, and it will give you something to reflect upon as you go through the remaining sections.

Section 2 looks at people who tend to come out second-best and explains why they act like they do. It describes some character traits that you'll definitely want to avoid.

Section 3 sets forth 20 well-defined techniques that will show you how to make your dreams a reality. They're all clear, concise, and to the point. All they need from you is some vim, vigor, and vitality.

The last section tells you how to put everything you know into a workable plan of action. By the time you reach the end of the book, you'll be chomping at the bit to get in the race with the swift and the strong.

MY ELEMENTS OF SUCCESS

1. WHAT I LIKE ABOUT MY JOB

_____

_____

_____

_____

2. GOOD BOOKS I'VE READ IN THE PAST YEAR

_____

_____

_____

_____

3. THINGS THAT MAKE ME HAPPY

_____

_____

_____

_____

MY ELEMENTS OF SUCCESS

4. THINGS I'M THANKFUL FOR

_____

_____

_____

_____

2. MY CLOSEST FRIENDS

_____

_____

_____

_____

3. FEARS I HAVE CONQUERED

_____

_____

_____

_____

WHAT WINNERS AVOID

You should first understand that being fair to middling is not a life sentence. You can be a consistent winner. But it takes a lot of hope, faith, and hard work. The very idea of wanting to be successful can produce a force of its own that's strong enough to break the shackles of inertia and get a person back on track.

Without hard work and dedication, down-and-outers will probably never reach the levels of success they've always dreamed of. They'll continue to be hobbled by the crippling traits and bad attitudes that louse up their lives.

Nonwinners behave in fairly predictable ways. They generally try something, make a mess of it, and then dwell on their mistakes instead of trying to learn something from them. They feel hurt, frustrated, and depressed. Instead of looking forward to the future, they watch their self-confidence fade like a five-dollar shirt.

People usually miss the mark because they procrastinate, lack motivation, refuse to plan, are unable to translate thought into action, and have a hard time getting along with other people. They lack creativity, leadership, and perseverance. They're unable to prepare for or take advantage of opportunities that appear before them. And they seek immediate gratification for almost everything they do.

Sounds bad, doesn't it? If you feel bummed out now, you probably have a dim view of your chances for success. But don't give up hope, because for every weakness that's listed below, there is a way to get rid of it and put strength in its place. See if you can't come up with some constructive ideas of your own as you plow through this list of frustrating traits.

FEAR

Some people are afraid of the responsibility that comes with decisive action. They're afraid to experiment with new behaviors or to confront new people and new situations. They're afraid of change and often think up disastrous scenarios to justify their devotion to the status quo. They explain their inertia by saying that doom is just around the corner.

They dwell on their past foul-ups, failures, and setbacks and spend precious hours thinking up reasons why they happened. To them, a mistake is a humiliation that must be avoided at all costs. They don't see it as an honest appraisal of what they did, or as an objective statement of what they need to do to improve.

Sometimes the possibility of winning scares the daylights out of them. They're afraid their success will dictate new expectations and awesome responsibilities that they won't be able to handle. Failure becomes a self-defense mechanism that allows them to avoid the visibility and accountability that comes with success.

PESSIMISM

Winners see answers for every problem; losers see problems for every answer. Winners say, "It may be difficult, but it's possible." Losers say, "It may be possible, but it's too difficult."

When pessimists make up their minds to do something, it usually involves so many don'ts — like don't smoke, don't eat, or don't be late — that they seldom get a clear picture of what it is they're supposed to do.

Their glasses are always half empty, instead of half full. Their days are always partly cloudy, never partly sunny. The wind is always in their face, the sun never shines on their parades.

Pessimists are basically insecure and tend to focus on their limitations instead of their strengths. They *expect* bad things to happen to them. Instead of taking positive steps to promote success, they lapse into a state of hopelessness, despair, and stagnation.

They cultivate and hold sarcastic thoughts about everything and everyone around them. They love to gossip, and will go out of their way to dig up dirt about someone else. They don't pay much attention to their thoughts when bad things happen, but invariably, their negative thoughts lead to negative action.

Instead of asking themselves what they can do better, they keep harping about the things they've done wrong.

BAD HABITS

Nonproductive people have a lot of bad habits, but the worst one is their habit of underachieving; of never living up to their potential in personal or professional relationships. They can't deal with failure, so they either take on easy tasks where they know they'll be successful, or they take on impossible tasks where no one can criticize them if they drop the ball. They have never disciplined themselves to develop winning habits—like patience, persistence, and perseverance—that could enhance their efforts and improve their lives.

Change is difficult to accomplish. It takes hard work and know-how, and it doesn't happen overnight. The natural tendency among stick-in-the-muds is to resist new habits that could bring about change. They would rather stay with old, ineffective habits and say, "I'm hopeless, I'll never change."

PROCRASTINATION

Procrastinators make a regular habit of postponing important tasks that they should be working on. It's the main reason why they're never at the head of the pack.

They try to hide in a fantasy world where they will no longer have to make tough decisions about the future. They postpone change even though it would improve their prospects for a better life. And no matter how demoralizing and draining it is, they still feel secure in whatever they're presently doing. To them, change would be more painful than doing nothing.

Procrastinators can recognize problems all right, but they have a hard time turning those problems into opportunities. They focus too much on negative aspects and not enough on the positive steps they need to take to get off dead center.

NO CONTROL

A sense of control is the litmus test for success. When successful people feel that things are starting to go wrong, they act quickly to identify their mistakes and look for solutions. They form new plans, deal directly with obstacles, and reach out for advice.

Muddlers, on the other hand, generally move without direction and without definite goals. That makes it hard for them to recognize problems or to come up with workable solutions. Instead of taking control of their lives, they blame their lack of progress on the turn of the cards and say there is nothing they can do to make things better.

Even making small decisions, like figuring out what clothes to wear or what to eat for lunch, gets very difficult. People who seem lost in space would rather turn control over to others and avoid any responsibility for making decisions. Many of them are already dependent on others for the management of their affairs.

People who don't take control of their lives fail to recognize that they are solely responsible for the thoughts, feelings, choices, and actions that cause them pain. They voluntarily allow their feelings of anger, guilt, and anxiety to control their behavior and determine their future.

NO LEARNING

Some people are unsuccessful because they can't comprehend difficult concepts or analyze new situations quickly, clearly, or incisively. Many can't even come up with sound, practical judgments about day-to-day events they read or hear about in the news. Some of them don't even understand the basic competencies that are needed to make a decent living. The most unfortunate ones lack the desire to gain new knowledge or to learn what they need to know to be successful. Many of them fail to reach the top of their occupation or profession because they refuse to learn new skills.

These people lack the desire to build their vocabulary, or to develop good reading and writing skills. They lack inquiring minds and have very short ranges of interests. Many of them have either forgotten how to learn or they think they're too old to try new things. It's a real tussle to get them to engage in mental aerobics of any kind.

NO DIRECTION

People who have a habit of floundering need others to motivate and lead them. Without outside help, they float through life like rudderless ships. They usually have non-existent or poorly-defined goals, so it's hard for them to know where they've been, where they are, or where they're heading. Instead of responding to a problem with a goal, they respond with fear and uncertainty.

They worry so much about what could go wrong that they don't have time to think about opportunities they could be looking forward to and preparing for. They express their frustration in wish lists and statements like, "I wish I had," or "I wish I could be."

They have a hard time seeing themselves as being successful because they don't know what it takes to be a winner. They can't set priorities because they don't know what's important and what's not. They look for excuses instead of answers.

NO COMMITMENT

Winners say, "Let me do it for you." Losers say, "That's not my job."

It's very rare for people to find a perfect match between their values, interests, personality, and style of operation and the jobs they have to do. Winners will try to adjust to their responsibilities and do the best job possible. Nonwinners, on the other hand, are generally unwilling to make new commitments or to learn new responsibilities. They use the apparent mismatch of skills and tasks as a rationalization for not being successful.

Fence-straddlers usually don't commit themselves to their tasks, because they don't believe they have what it takes to get them done. They're not very excited about the potential benefits, nor are they concerned about poor results. They usually maintain an indifferent attitude, which is often reflected in the way they interact with other people. And by not being accountable for their behavior, they also fail to become its primary creative force.

NO MOTIVATION

People who lack motivation are generally not concerned about doing better because they think they're doing all right where they are. They have no realistic notions of how they could improve if they wanted to. They have a hard time getting motivated because they have no desire to satisfy any goals or objectives. They don't see how accomplishing a short-term resolution, like changing a bad habit or learning a new skill, will make things any different for them. They lack the incentive to grow socially, financially, spiritually, or intellectually and are content to live their lives in mediocrity.

NO SELF-ESTEEM

Lack of confidence and poor self-esteem are the hallmarks of failure. The timid, fearful soul who is totally lacking in confidence and is completely possessed by a tragic flair for failure, stands in sharp contrast to the self-confident winner who strives daily to succeed and be happy. The fainthearted lose because they expect to lose. Just getting through the day is as much as many of them ever hope to achieve. They don't get their hopes up because they don't want to face the anxiety that comes with losing again.

They project themselves as losers by behaving in ways that reinforce their failure identity. They walk, talk, dress, look, listen, and react to life like losers. It's a total development that other people find easy to identify. It's also their way of getting the attention and sympathy they so often need.

Generally, when people lose their self-esteem, they also lose their self-respect. They are less responsibile, their standards of behavior go down, they don't work as hard as they once did, and they are not as faithful to friends, family, or employers.

NO PERSEVERANCE

People who approach life half-heartedly usually lack willpower, good work habits, organizational skills, and the ability to set goals. Hard work is for many of them an alien concept. They are not self-starters and do not diligently seek the skills they need to be successful.

It's hard for them to rely on their own resources and abilities because they don't know what they are, and they don't have enough gumption to find out. They would rather rely on other people to steer them in the right direction and tell them what to do.

The old saying, "when the going gets tough, the tough get going", does not apply to this group.

POOR PERCEPTION

Nonwinners tend to focus on negative details, so every crisis is seen as a potentially disastrous situation in which they will fail again, lose what they already have, and fall further in the hole. They see themselves as living in a grim, glum, and gloomy swamp.

It's hard for people with poor self-images to recall past successes or truly satisfying times of any kind. And since they have a hard time looking back at the good things they've done, they find it just as difficult looking forward to see what they could do in the future.

People who can't see how or why they screwed up, have a tough time admitting their mistakes or accepting blame when things go wrong. And because they can't (or won't) face up to their errors, they also find it difficult to come up with any solutions.

Short-sighted people have problems trying to overcome obstacles because they can't always see them. Their focus is so scattered that when they do encounter barriers, they don't know what to do to get by them. They see too many things to do, and they know they're not going to be able to do any of them very well. It's like trying to meet an income tax deadline and solve a family crisis at the same time.

WISHFUL THINKING

Many people have off-the-wall ideas about what it takes to be successful. They would rather drop a nickel in a wishing well than commit themselves to an idea and develop a plan for carrying it out. They would rather wish upon a star than develop goals and objectives with starting points and deadlines.

They like to think big. But their great expectations usually lead to even bigger disappointments. That's because they can't see the advantage of taking small, easily-attainable steps that would help build the momentum they need to succeed.

Wishful thinkers have a distorted view of what's real and what's not. Instead of stating their problems honestly and confronting them directly, they either exaggerate or understate them. They think their success will come from chance, luck, or the actions of other people. They don't think there is anything they can do by themselves to get the results they want.

RELIANCE ON LUCK

Some people discount the importance of hard work and perseverance and rely instead on the mysteries of chance. They rationalize their incompetence and blame their lack of success on the odds and the gods. They have to believe in luck, or else they couldn't explain the success of those they don't like.

The American poet and philosopher Ralph Waldo Emerson commented on how winners and losers reacted differently to random events. He said, "Shallow people believe in luck. Wise and strong people believe in cause and effect."

SUBJECT TO STRESS

Many people are routinely thrown for a loss whenever they encounter obstacles. They end up as frequent victims of stress because so few of them know anything about the techniques of stress management, or have taken the time to develop coping skills.

Anxious people create their own stress by blaming themselves and jumping to guilt-ridden conclusions whenever things go wrong. When pressure starts building, they get angry and frustrated and lose sight of their long-range outcomes. The more pressure they are under to do well, the more likely they are to make mistakes. They haven't learned how to shift their focus away from themselves and on to the automatic functions of their task where it can be defused.

They intensify their stress and increase their misery by bemoaning their circumstances and harping about their hardships. Their negative emotions make other stress-reducing activities like reading, writing, reminiscing, or meditating just as ineffective.

NEED FOR GRATIFICATION

People who go up like a rocket and come down like a rock seldom get turned on by the processes that lead to success. They expect things to happen right away, and if their desires are not met at the drop of a hat, they lose interest, discard their pursuits, and seek gratification from other sources. Perseverance is not one of their strong suits.

People who only think about results are too wrapped up in life's immediate rewards to recognize long-term benefits where the potential payoff is equal to or greater than the risk. They only see short-term gains that aren't worth the effort. The perceived drudgery of their immediate task prevents them from discovering the delight that comes from long-term, worthwhile endeavors.

These people tend to overgeneralize single failures into forecasts of gloom and defeat. Instead of learning from some bonehead move and getting on to better things, they abandon their cause and turn their attention to a whole new set of tasks.

POOR INTERPERSONAL SKILLS

Self-centered people are reluctant to commit themselves to others or to build a network of supportive relationships. It's hard for them to believe in others or to nurture other people's dreams. Instead of doing to others as they would have others do to them, they try to take advantage of others before others have a chance to take advantage of them. They see no practical benefit in helping other people and are often disappointed when favors and gifts are not reciprocated.

They usually have a distorted idea of how other people view them and find it difficult, if not impossible, to see themselves through the eyes of others. They don't listen to criticism, and they don't internalize what others try to tell them. Instead of asking for solutions, they counterattack, offer excuses, or retreat into silence.

At the same time, self-centered people are generally quick to criticize or condemn others when things don't go their way. They seldom give honest, sincere appreciation, because it's hard for them to become genuinely interested in what other people do.

They like to be the center of attention, seldom encourage others to talk about themselves, and are quick to jump out of conversations that center on other people's interests.

THE ROAD AHEAD

So much for the commonplace. Now it's time to turn your attention to techniques that help make people winners. Section 3 contains 20 surefire methods for leaving the dull world of the mediocre and hustling on over to the highly attractive world of the successful. You won't be disappointed.

HOW TO BE A WINNER

Winners try to be successful in every facet of life, as parents, spouses, citizens, neighbors, workers, and friends. They try to make the most of their minds and bodies by identifying their talents, skills, and abilities and applying them where they will do the most good.

They do their best to strengthen the character traits on which all success depends. These traits include, among others, joy, faith, poise, courage, honesty, humility, patience, optimism, enthusiasm, confidence, and cheerfulness.

Success in life is more a matter of concentration and perseverance than it is of talent or opportunity. Winners don't pray for tasks equal to their powers, they pray for powers equal to their tasks. They know they can do anything if they stick to it long enough.

This section contains 20 time-tested strategies for becoming a winner. There are undoubtedly a lot more things you could do and still be effective. Those that are presented here are just some of the more familiar ones. If you can add to the list, then by all means, feel free to do so.

These techniques are not presented in any particular order of importance. Some may be harder to do than others, and some may have more relevance to your unique situation. But they're all guaranteed to work as long as you add a few shots of motivation, commitment, and energy.

WIN A FEW

Start out by taking small steps that are easily attainable. It will boost your confidence, teach you to be patient, and give you the momentum you need to reach goals and objectives that are of greater consequence.

Tackle small tasks that can give you a quick sense of accomplishment and not take more than 15 to 20 minutes to do. Select a variety of tasks that can provide both immediate and delayed gratification. That way, you can spread your results over a longer period of time and still have something to look forward to every day.

Go for a walk, clean your garage, or jot down notes for the novel you want to write. Plant a garden full of things that are easy to grow like squash, pumpkins, potatoes, carrots, and radishes.

Nothing breeds success like success, as long as you keep the process going. Just don't penalize yourself if one of your tasks fizzles out. You don't want to overgeneralize a single unfortunate event into an overall forecast of gloom and despair. Discipline yourself to accept the loss with equanimity, then move on to other events that still hold the promise of success.

BE HAPPY

Sebastian Chamfort, the French satirist said, "The most utterly lost of all days is one in which you have not once laughed." He obviously knew the value of laughter in relieving stress and promoting gaiety.

A good laugh is more than just a great tension reliever. It aids digestion, improves concentration, raises your pulse rate, strengthens your muscles, lowers your blood pressure, stimulates your heart and endocrine system, and activates the creative center of your brain. Three to five minutes of hearty laughter is the equivalent of three strenuous minutes on a rowing machine.

The deeper the giggles, the greater the exercise of the internal muscles in your lungs and abdomen. A hearty dose of laughter will do wonders to relieve the muscle pain of arthritis, rheumatism, or other related conditions.

Joy and laughter affect the way you feel about what you have to do and consequently, the way you do it. If you're happy, you'll get done sooner, have fewer problems, and have better results. A humorous approach to your tasks will increase your creativity, reduce your resistance to change, and provide you with a storehouse of useful ideas. You will feel less threatened by the prospect of stress and find it easier to respond to troublesome demands.

Develop a happy, healthy attitude by thinking happy thoughts. Seek happiness in humorous books, hilarious movies, and side-splitting TV programs. Let your hair down, and allow yourself the pleasure of laughing at things you think are funny. Make a habit of smiling. It will improve your disposition and exercise your facial muscles. Positive emotions like joy, love, hope, faith, and confidence will increase the number of immune cells in your body and contribute to a number of other beneficial chemical changes that will help you live longer. As Mary Pettibone Poole said, "They who laugh, last."

VISUALIZE

Use positive illusions, like fantasies and daydreams, to increase your capacity for productive work and create feelings of well-being and happiness. Entertain illusions of unfounded optimism, exaggerated feelings of control, and unrealistically positive views of yourself. Become the jolly green giant. It's healthy and easy to do, and it can provide you with a ready source of fun and encouragement.

Create a vision in your mind's eye of what you realistically have to do to be successful. Hold the picture and focus on the details. Let your subconscious draw your vision into your memory bank. Then pull it back into view whenever you have to overcome an obstacle or remind yourself of the goals you set.

Zero in on a single positive detail in your search for success, like the smile that will be on your face when you reach a significant milestone. Let your focus spread until you see your entire mission in a positive way. Practice this simple technique several times a day and pretty soon your whole world will begin to look sunny and warm.

Think about where you want to be a week, a month, or a year from today. See yourself as having successfully achieved the task you're working on right now. Let your vision be your guide and try to make your goal a reality.

PERSEVERE

If a goal is worth having, it's worth pursuing. Shrug off the little mickey-mouse things that irritate you, and make up your mind to enjoy what you're doing. Concentrate on the tasks that will bear the most fruit.

Translate your thoughts into action, and do your best even when you'd rather not.

Discipline yourself to make sound, practical judgments about your progress. Sweep aside tentative goals, and go to work on those that really mean something. Work on the ideal and make adjustments as you go along. Plan for gradual improvement rather than quantum leaps. And don't be so results-oriented that you lose interest in your goals whenever your performance falls short of hoped-for levels of satisfaction. Learn to delay gratification.

Don't consider a sudden lapse into a bad habit as a defeat. Treat it as an emergency that requires immediate attention. Figure out what caused the miscue so you'll know what to watch for in the future. Get back on track by renewing your commitment to be a winner. Make immediate plans for recovery. Ask for help if you need it.

PRIORITIZE

The greatest measure of success is to be able to accomplish your own goals and objectives, while at the same time helping others achieve theirs.

Lend a helping hand whenever you can. But don't devote so much time to other people's needs and desires that you lose touch with your own. Giving until it hurts is not a true measure of charity.

Know which of your tasks are urgent, which are important, and which are essential to your success. Separate your *have tos* from your *choose tos*.

Steer clear of busy work when you can, and try not to let others waste your time. Time is a very precious commodity, and once it's gone you can never get it back.

Ask yourself if what you're doing really contributes to your long-range goals or short-term objectives. If you're not sure, then you should take another look at the way you set your priorities.

Here's an exercise that will help. Turn to page 31 and write down—in order of their importance—ten things you know you have to do to be successful. Add a comment after each one why you think it's an important task. When you're done, come back here and get ready to take advantage of life's opportunities.

THE TEN MOST IMPORTANT TASKS IN MY LIFE
IN ORDER OF THEIR IMPORTANCE

1. _____

2. _____

3. _____

4. _____

5. _____

6. _____

7. _____

8. _____

9. _____

10. _____

BE PREPARED

Good luck is the goldbricker's estimate of a hard-worker's success. You only get lucky if you are prepared to take advantage of the opportunities that come your way. You can't win the lottery if you don't buy a ticket. You can't make a sale if you're not available when the customer calls. And you can't find your heart's desire if you never get out of your tree house.

Have your goals and objectives before you. Know how much time you have available. Lay out the tools you need so they'll be readily accessible. Practice the skills that are required. Know what obstacles lie in wait and try to predict the probability of their occurrence.

Prospect for opportunities as enthusiastically as you would prospect for gold. Tickle the creative corners of your imagination and come up with a list of circumstances that might contribute to your success. Include things like changes in the weather, changes in the stock market, or changes in your economic status; anything that might help you in a positive way.

Once you've identified some realistic opportunities, get set to take advantage of them as soon as they appear. Then, and only then, will you enjoy good luck.

TAKE CONTROL

Develop a strong personality and express it in everything you do. Project yourself as a winner in the way you walk, talk, dress, listen, and react to others.

Be decisive and do as much as you can by yourself. Do your own thinking and speak up for your own convictions. Write down the pros and cons of the choices you have to make. Weigh each alternative by the risk it carries and the promise it holds. Then make your own decision in quiet confidence. Be direct in your approach and accept full responsibility for your outcomes.

BE COURAGEOUS

Focus on opportunities instead of problems. Face threats head on and deal with them directly and effectively. Hammer out the courage you need to handle the future. Let your worries fade into refreshing thoughts of fun things to do. Prepare for each new day and look forward to it with anticipation.

Rocky Aoki, the founder of the Benihana of Tokyo restaurant chain said, "You only win if you're not afraid to lose." His success is a monument to his tenacity in going after a dream he really believed in.

Believe in yourself and strengthen your desire to succeed and be happy. Strive for continual growth, but don't lose sight of the things you have to do today. Don't be afraid to seek out new people and new situations. Have the courage to meet new challenges on your own terms. And remember that the surest way to avoid failure is to make up your mind to succeed.

TAKE A CHANCE

Look at every crisis as an opportunity to gain something, prove yourself, do well, and succeed.

Face up to tough decisions about the days ahead. If a change would offer the possibility of a brighter future, then go for it, no matter how painful it may be in the short haul. The security of having a job is meaningless if your insides are being torn apart because you're afraid to leave.

Ask yourself this question: "If I weren't already doing this, would I choose to do it now"?

No situation is worth the stress and resentment that comes from trying to justify why you're staying where you are. The world will not come to an end if you pack up and go on to something new. Get your facts straight, be clear on your position, know what you want to accomplish, and get on with it.

KNOW YOURSELF

The Swiss physicist Johann Zimmerman said, "Never lose sight of this important truth, that no one can be truly great until they have gained a knowledge of themselves."

Recognize your talents and skills and put them to good use wherever you can. Accept limitations if you have them, but don't let them get in the way of your progress.

Recall your past successes and failures with a willingness to forgive. Look for patterns of improvement and see if you've incorporated them where they'll do the most good. Keep a "victory list" of all the big and little accomplishments that have given you the most satisfaction. Review your list from time to time to remind yourself that you have succeeded in the past and can succeed again in the future.

Pay attention to your feelings because they're your greatest source of motivation. Keep a journal and describe how your emotions have influenced all your deeds and misdeeds. Every time you reflect on the good and bad things that happen to you, you'll get a better understanding of who you are and what you're trying to do. Keeping a journal is safe, personal, and easy to do anytime and anywhere. It reduces stress, promotes good mental health, and helps you make better decisions in your business and personal life.

BE RESPONSIBLE

Songwriter Irving Berlin said, "The toughest thing about success is that you've got to keep on being a success." There is no doubt that he met the challenge.

Success poses an awesome responsibility, and one that many people find too hard to handle. You shouldn't have a problem with it as long as you remember that you are the primary creative force behind your success. You just have to be accountable for your behavior and willing to accept the consequences of your actions.

Your choices shape your experiences and add form and substance to your life. If you make all the right choices, you won't have to worry about being successful. But if you make a mistake, admit it, accept the blame, and look for a remedy. The sooner you face up to an error, the easier it will be to find a solution. If you shirk responsibility, or argue about who's at fault, you'll get mired down in a morass of emotional sludge.

Make tough choices and then act decisively. Be responsible, but don't overpersonalize your involvement by thinking everything revolves around you. Don't jump to guilt-ridden conclusions or blame yourself for everything that goes wrong. And don't accept more responsibility for a situation than is warranted, or you'll weigh yourself down with a lot of unnecessary stress.

COMMIT YOURSELF

Promise yourself that you will break the bonds of mediocrity and do everything possible to fulfill your goals and objectives. Do more than just carry out certain acts that you think might lead to successful outcomes. Resolve instead to definitely become a winner. The acts will follow on their own.

Focus on doing things that will build your self-esteem and make you a better person. Get involved emotionally. Convince yourself that you can do almost anything. Avoid "don't" resolutions. They never give you a clear picture of what it is you're supposed to do anyway. All they do is remind you of what you're doing wrong.

Share your commitment with others and you'll be more apt to follow through on your good intentions. You'll think more about other people and they'll be more willing to help when you run into problems.

BUILD CHARACTER

Character is the personal standard of conduct, or base of acceptable behavior, on which you're judged by your peers. The essence of your character lies in your honesty, integrity, and moral strength.

Reputation is the opinion others have formed about you. You can't determine what other people say or think about you, but you can determine what they ought to say or think. Your reputation can be destroyed by slander, but your character can only be harmed by you. If you take care of your character, your reputation will take care of itself.

Build your character from the truths, principles, assumptions, and general laws that guide the world you live in. Be emotionally and intellectually honest with yourself and others. Show your self-respect by recognizing and practicing simple integrity. Be loyal to your companions, faithful to your ideals, and responsible for your behavior.

RELATE TO OTHERS

The *Golden Rule* is a powerful expression of human kindness, and it can have an enormous impact on your drive for success. All you have to do to make it work is help someone every day and give them what they need to be successful. They, in turn, will give you what you need to reach your goals and objectives.

Build a network of supportive relationships. Commit yourself to others. Respect them, believe in them, and nurture their dreams.

Be genuinely interested in other people. Talk about their interests and encourage them to talk about themselves. Be a good listener.

Refrain from criticizing, condemning, or complaining about other people. Encourage others to do their best. Give them honest, sincere appreciation when it's due. Make them feel important and do it sincerely. Be quick to smile.

Learn to handle criticism, and remember that those who offer it may be right. If they are, be straightforward in your acceptance and say, "You're right, I see your point."

Don't counterattack when others criticize, and don't offer excuses or retreat into silence. Be honest. If you don't agree, say so, and don't say you agree when you don't. Be quiet, listen to what is said, and use their suggestions where it can do the most good. If you need more information, ask for details and a possible solution. Don't be afraid to ask, "What specifically would you like me to do?"

THINK POSITIVELY

Be *for* things instead of against things. If a negative thought sneaks into your consciousness, chase it out and quickly substitute a positive one in its place. Act like your negative feelings aren't there and take positive steps to get back in a productive mood.

Accentuate the positive. Affirm your self-worth by responding positively to the good things that happen to you. Use self-esteem tools like exercise, meditation, relaxation, and positive self- talk to develop good feelings about yourself.

Having positive, nonegotistical views about yourself is more beneficial to your mental well-being than seeing your faults as clearly as others do. Exaggerated optimism and a sense of control will give you the strength and confidence you need to be a winner.

Feeling good about yourself will make you more acceptive of others. They, in turn, will recognize your optimism and will become willing partners in your quest for a better life.

Avoid labeling yourself as a ne'er-do-well when you make mistakes, and stop doing instant replays of your screw-ups. It's incriminating and demoralizing. If you mess up, just say so and let it go at that. Realize that although you may have dropped the ball a time or two, you're still a complex person with many dimensions. You're not a klutz.

Positive thinking will ignite a zest for living, make you more energetic, spontaneous, and enthusiastic, and provide the spark you need to set the world on fire.

PLAN YOUR FUTURE

Peter Drucker, the management expert, said, "The best way to predict the future is to create it." You've got what it takes, so do it.

Start with a purpose in life. Then establish a goal with a starting point and a deadline, and figure out what steps you have to take to accomplish it. Narrow your focus by limiting the number of things you have to do, then do each of them well.

Be realistic. A wish is one thing. But commiting yourself to an idea, setting goals and objectives, and developing and following a plan involves much, much more.

The best goals are achievable, believable, and limited in scope. They should excite you, motivate you, and direct you toward the satisfaction of a specific need. Their purpose is to help you grow socially, physically, financially, spiritually, and intellectually. If you don't have goals and objectives, you forfeit control over your life. Your future may then depend on the fickle finger of fate.

Take a few minutes and think about your goals. Then turn to page 38 and list your five most important ones in order of their importance. Write down your anticipated results and hoped-for completion dates. Then go to work on your objectives.

When you develop your list of short-term objectives, be sure to keep in mind your long-range goals that take three to five years to carry out. You'll see how polishing off a one-year resolution (changing a bad habit or learning a new skill) will bring you one step closer to reaching a long-range goal (starting a new career or being promoted in a current one). You'll be more motivated to accomplish your one-year objectives if you can see how they fit into your overall program.

FIVE MAJOR GOALS OF MINE IN ORDER
OF THEIR IMPORTANCE

1. *GOAL:* _____

   Completion Date: _____

   Anticipated Results: _____

2. *GOAL:* _____

   Completion Date: _____

   Anticipated Results: _____

3. *GOAL:* _____

   Completion Date: _____

   Anticipated Results: _____

4. *GOAL:* _____

   Completion Date: _____

   Anticipated Results: _____

5. *GOAL:* _____

   Completion Date: _____

   Anticipated Results: _____

Refine your goals from time to time to make sure your life is heading down the right track. Don't become so preoccupied with day-to-day problems and challenges that you lose sight of your long-term aspirations.

BROADEN YOUR BASE

Your progress toward a successful future is affected by the assumptions you make about current economic conditions, anticipated business developments, or changes in your social life. Assumptions are gut feelings you have about what will happen in the next few weeks, months, or years.

Keep your assumptions up-to-date by broadening the basis upon which they're founded. Combine your ideas, rearrange them, modify them, magnify them, minify them, exaggerate them, reverse them, turn them upside down, or transfer them to different applications. Substitute new ideas for old, or take old ideas and put them to new uses.

CULTIVATE YOUR MIND

Cultivate an inquiring mind and a broad range of interests. Seek an environment that will nurture your quest for knowledge. Learn something new every day.

Develop a realistic understanding of the crafts and skills that relate to your occupation. Build your vocabulary by taking a few minutes out of every day to look up the definition of four new words. Develop good reading and writing skills. If you're an average reader and read 15 minutes a day, you can read the equivalent of 20 new books a year.

Develop additional knowledge in areas that have always appealed to you. Do the same in areas that are outside your current fields of interest. Learn about the world you're in. Study biology, geography, and weather forecasting.

Build your self-confidence by developing new skills. Try a new recipe, learn to perform a magic trick, or start a new hobby, like painting, woodworking, or stamp collecting.

Establish new relationships with people who share similar interests and skills.

Get involved in some mental activity that relates to your physical condition. Take tap dancing lessons. Join an aerobics class. Enter an orienteering race.

CONTROL YOUR EMOTIONS

Practice psychic self-control. Know when to be assertive and when to be passive. Learn to handle anger quickly and effectively. Know when to suppress anger and when to vent it in an appropriate way, like cursing, hitting a pillow, or counting to 10. Watch out for anger's kissing cousins, anxiety and depression, because they can foul you up just as bad.

Stay in control. Use positive self-talk to keep from losing your cool when you encounter disturbing events or ugly words. Learn how to confront other people without getting into violent arguments. It's okay to tell others that you're angry, but give them usable information so both of you can do something about the situation.

Change your mood if it interferes with your progress. Do something that will restore your positive attitude. Go shopping, get some exercise, read a good book, or call on a friend. Take a drive, take a walk, or spend time in a park or garden. Then come back to your task and give it your complete attention.

If you're going to rant and rave, do it in the privacy of your home. Otherwise, pamper yourself, plan a vacation, or do something that will make you happy. Create order out of chaos by cleaning out a closet or putting your financial affairs in order. Discipline yourself to make choices.

BE A PROBLEM SOLVER

Deal directly with any problems that might interfere with your progress toward being a winner. State the problem as clearly as you can. Absorb as much information as you can about it. Look at it from as many viewpoints as possible. Try to identify the opportunities it presents.

Let your information bubble and boil like stew so all the different ingredients can blend together. Then focus on one simple, realistic, clear-cut solution that stands out above all others. Don't waste your time on idealized fantasies. See if potential rewards are equal to or greater than anticipated risks.

Test and refine your solution with a plan of action that has a goal, a purpose, and a list of milestones. Don't be discouraged if your first approach comes up short. Consider it an unplanned outcome, an opportunity to try again. Then recycle the process if you have to, and look for another solution.

Be a part of the answer, not a part of the problem. Have a program instead of an excuse. See an answer for every problem, instead of a problem for every answer.

Problem solving requires hard work, motivation, good work habits, and stick-to-itiveness. If you're lacking any of the necessary qualities, take immediate steps to acquire them through study and application.

Practice solving problems that you read or hear about in the news. Describe social, political, economic, or religious issues from different perspectives. Devise alternative solutions that would be acceptable to opposing parties. Outline steps that could be taken to carry out each solution. Describe potential barriers and opportunities. Make a list of the kinds of consequences you'd expect if each of your solutions were actually put into effect.

GO FOR IT

Now you know what it takes to be successful and you've got the resources to do it. You've got this book full of suggestions, but you've got two more things that are far more important. You've got an good mind and a healthy body. You can't do everything, but you can do something. And in order to do the something that really counts, you need to put your mind and body to work in a winning plan of action. The next section tells you how.

A PLAN OF ACTION

The pathway to success is well-defined and waiting to be traveled. Start with a single-minded desire to become something better; to live well, laugh often, and love much. Express your desire in a set of goals that you can complete in a day, a week, a month, a year, or over your lifetime. Acknowledge the benefits you'll receive by reaching those goals. Then get fired-up to pursue them.

Devise and carry out an effective, on-going process for achieving your goals. Lay down a series of milestones that will earmark your progress. Set some starting times and ending dates. Adopt some realistic measures of achievement. Tie it all together in a program that's easy to follow and fun to work on. If you need technical assistance, turn to other books in the DO IT! Success Series, especially *Plan For Success*.

Act quickly, but don't expect immediate gratification, because winning takes time. Recognize and utilize the power of patience.

Strive to be a winner in every single aspect of your life. Think of each part of your existence as being an individual stone on the pathway to success. Cement each stone as you go along. Become a winning spouse, parent, sibling, friend, lawyer, carpenter, or whatever. Follow that accomplishment by becoming successful in another capacity. Blend the elements of good living into each of your daily tasks.

Tax your staying power. Discipline yourself to keep pressing physically and mentally to reach your goals. Be conscious of the fact that as long as you strive for the best, the best will come your way.

Your plan of action can be summarized in this definition from the St. Louis Rotary Club.

Success is in the way you walk the paths of life each day;
  It's in the little things you do, and in the things you say.
Success is not in getting rich, or rising high to fame.
  It's not alone in winning goals, which all men hope to claim.

Success is being big of heart, and clean and broad of mind;
  It's being faithful to your friends, and to the stranger, kind.
It's in the children whom you love, and all they learn from you;
  Success depends on character, and everything you do.

You've waited long enough. Now it's time to get to work. You know what you have to do. ***DO IT!***

INDEX

INDEX

accountability: 34
adventurous: 10
aesthetic needs: 2
Aoki, Rocky: 33
Aristotle: 11
assumptions: 39
attitude, happy: 29
awareness: 8

bad habits: 19, 30
basic skills: 20
being
 a problem solver: 40
 courageous: 32
 prepared: 32
 responsible: 34
belongingness and love needs: 2
Berlin, Irving: 34
Borge, Victor: 13
broadening one's base: 39
building character: 35
busy work: 30

Chamfort, Sebastian: 28
chance, mysteries of: 24
chances, taking: 33
change: 19, 32
character: 35
cognitive needs: 2
commitment: 35

lack of: 21
confidence: 27
control
 lack of: 20
 taking: 32
controlling emotions: 40
Coolidge Calvin: 8
courage: 32
crises: 23, 33
 management of: 24
criticism: 25, 36

definition
 of losers: 1
 of success: 43–44
 of winners: 1
direction, lack of: 21
"don't" resolutions: 35
Drucker, Peter: 37

efficiency: 10
Emerson, Ralph Waldo: 24
emotions, control of: 40
esteem needs: 2

failure identity: 22
failures: 33
fantasies and daydreams: 29
fear: 18
 mastering: 11

feelings: 34
fickle finger of fate: 20
Ford, Henry: 7
friendliness: 10
friendship: 10
future, planning for: 37

garden: 28
giving: 5, 30
  manner of: 5
goals: 43
  nature of: 37
  and objectives: 22
going for it: 41
Golden Rule: 9, 35
gratification: 30
  delayed: 28
  need for: 25
guiding: 6

habits
  bad: 19, 30
  constructive: 10
happiness: 8, 28
happy attitude: 29
Hunt, J. H. Leigh: 13

illusions, positive: 29
immortality: 11
important tasks: 30
interpersonal skills: 25

journal: 34

knowledge, of self: 33

Lamb, Charles: 12
laughing: 12, 43
laughter, benefits of: 28
learning, lack of: 20
lightheartedness: 13
living
  forever: 11

well: 5, 43
loving much: 13, 43
luck: 32
  reliance on: 24

Maslow, Abraham: 2
measures of achievement: 43
mediocrity: 35
milestones: 43
mistakes: 18
motivation, lack of: 21

needs
  aesthetic: 2
  belongingness and love: 2
  cognitive: 2
  esteem: 2
  physiological: 2
  safety: 2
  self-actualization: 2
nonwinners
  behavior of: 17
  characteristics of: 17
  definition of: 1

objectives, nature of: 37
one's self, being: 9
opportunities: 32, 40

parachutes: 7
pathway to success: 43
patience: 8, 27
  power of: 43
perception, poor: 23
perseverance: 25, 27, 29–30
  lack of: 22
persistence: 8
personality: 32
pessimism: 18
Peterson, Wilferd A: 5
physiological needs: 2
plan of action: 40, 43
planning one's future: 37

Poole, Mary Pettibone: 13
positive
  illusions: 29
  personality: 36
  thinking: 37
power of patience: 43
prepared, being: 32
priorities: 21, 30
problem solving: 40
  practice in: 41
procrastination: 19
prospecting: 32
psychic self-control: 40
purpose: 37

reading: 6
  and writing skills: 39
relating to others: 35
relationships, supportive: 36
relaxing: 7
reputation: 35
resolutions: 37
resources: 41
responsibility: 34
results-oriented: 30
risk: 32
Rochefoucauld, Francois: 9
Runyan, Damon: 1

safety needs: 2
self-actualization needs: 2
self-concept: 2
self-confidence: 39
self-control, psychic: 40
self-esteem: 35
  lack of: 22
self-knowledge: 33
self-respect: 35
  loss of: 22
self-talk: 40
selfhood: 9
sense
  of accomplishment: 28

of control: 20
small tasks: 28
St. Louis Rotary Club: 43
Stanley, Bessie Anderson: 5, 12
strategies, winning: 27
stress: 33
  victims of: 24
study: 39
subconscious: 29
success: 33, 34
  definition of: 43–44
  elements of: 5
  pathway to: 43
success, past: 33

taking
  chances: 33
  control: 32
thankful, being: 9
thinking: 7
  positive: 36
  wishful: 23
tough decisions: 33
true gift: 5
Twain, Mark: 6

unplanned outcomes: 41
urgent tasks: 30

victory list: 34
visualize: 29
vocabulary: 20, 39

want
  acquisition: 3
  affiliation: 3
  altruistic: 3
  curiosity: 3
  power: 3
  prestige: 3
wants, needs, and desires: 2, 3
win a few: 27

winners
  characteristics of: 27
  definition of: 1
wish lists: 21
wishful thinking: 23
wishing well: 23
working: 6

young people: 11
young, staying: 11

Zimmerman Johann: 33

—Notes—

—Notes—

—Notes—

—Notes—